ADHD and OCD Workbook for kids, parents and teachers too

By Michael R. Basso

I0417596

Edited by Dorothy Scarfone

First Edition

ISBN-10: 1456402315

About the Author

Dr. Michael R. Basso has been the author and coauthor of several children's books which are focused upon teaching children, parents and educators about people with disabilities.

Michael has significant experience as college level educator in psychology at Yale University and the University of Connecticut and well as being a leader in quality and reliability engineering and management in industry. His experience also includes being a consultant, researcher, and newspaper columnist. Michael is the president of the Connecticut Holistic Health Association.

Dr. Basso has a Ph.D. in professional psychology and biomedical systems, an MS in engineering science, and an MBA with a focus in executive leadership and an interdisciplinary Professional Development Diploma in pathophysiology, neural systems, and education. He also holds a BS in electrical engineering. Michael is certified in quality and reliability engineering and quality auditing, as well as a variety of health related areas.

About the Editor

Dorothy lives in New York with Frankie who has Down Syndrome. She has a daughter, Sandra, another son, Mark, and four grandchildren. Dorothy earned an Associates Degree at the Latin-American Institute in Manhattan and her paralegal certificate at Manhattanville College. She now works as a legal secretary/paralegal for a law firm in Greenwich, CT.

Dorothy was a literacy volunteer for many years starting when her children were in elementary school. She has continued to volunteer to teach English to the new wave of immigrants in her native village, Port Chester, NY. She also has been a member of the parish counsel of her church helping to establish goals for the parish. Presently, she is on a committee at her church which reaches out to the elderly. She was also a member of the Board of Directors of Don Bosco Community Center in Port Chester, NY.

Dorothy is also on the Board of Directors of the Tamarack Tower Foundation in Port Chester, NY as well as corresponding secretary for the TTF. She is also on the Board of Directors of the South East Consortium for Special Services, Inc., located in Mamaroneck, NY.

Please be advised that this book is not meant for the diagnosis and/or treatment of any disease. Parents or guardians are advised to consider seeking the advice of an expert whom they trust and feel safe with.

"Joey, I had trouble sleeping again last night. It was really weird, it was like I had to memorize all the presidents that there ever were – I couldn't stop it."

"That is weird, sis. It reminds me of when you were a little girl and you would wash your hands twenty times a day.

"Then you got really odd, Joanne – not only did you avoid the cracks in the sidewalk, like some other kids do.

You had to count the empty squares in every drain on every street."

6

"Well, you're weird too – you get soooo hyper when you study. You fidget, you move from chair to chair."

"Well, you should see me in school."

"Oh, gosh, what now, Joey?"

"Sometimes, I can't concentrate at all. We were doin math on the board the other day and

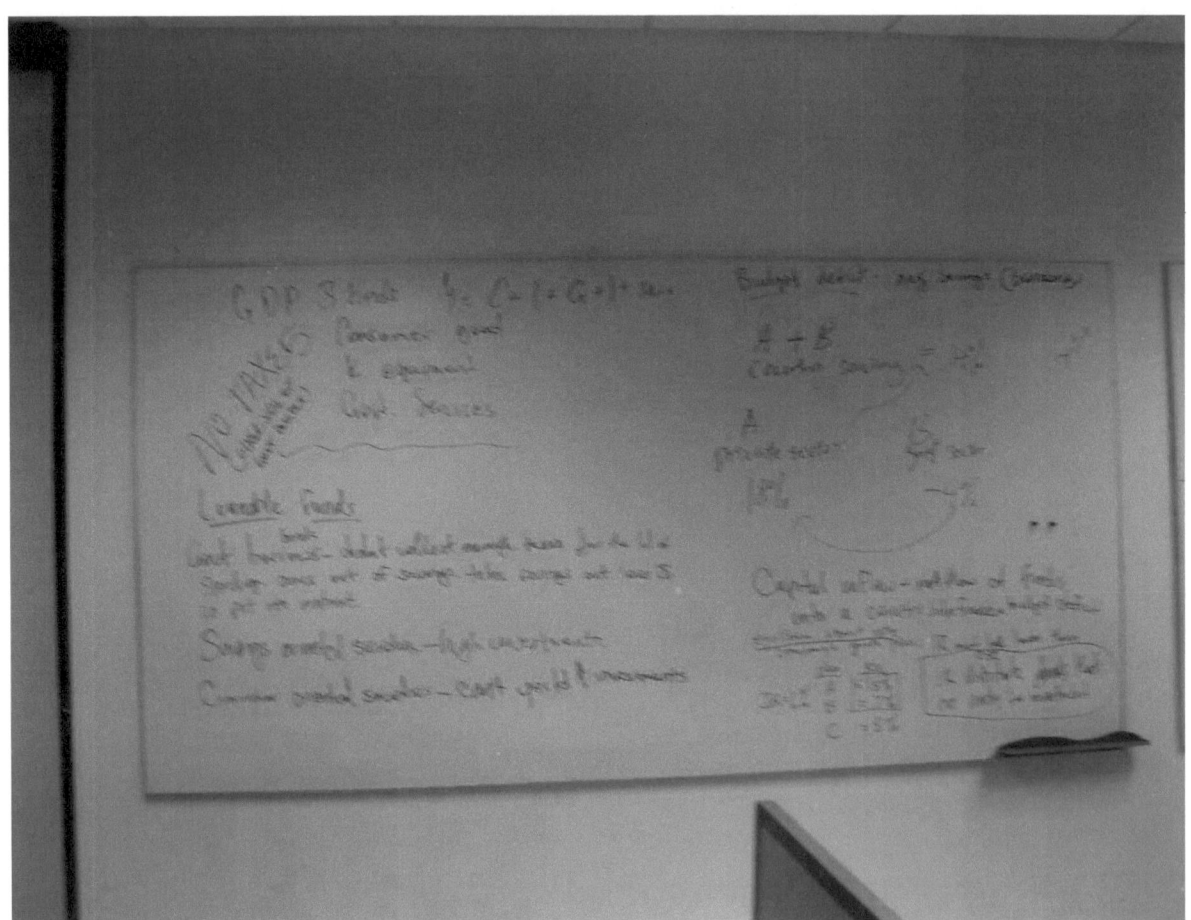

the more I tried, the harder it was to focus on the board and the math problems."

$$E=mc^2$$

'What!'

"We are a weird family – dad even has that Tourette thing, he twitches sometimes and yells things out! In school they said that Childhood OCD, Tourette Syndrome and ADHD sometimes happen in the same families – cause of some Gene thing."

"You mean those little things that make our hair a certain color, our bodies a certain height and even makes our voice a certain way?"

"Yep."

 They also say that chemicals in their brains might be different – like that sero ton in stuff we learned about on TV."

"You got it."

"You know, brother, you seem to get even worse when you start eating that sweet junk food and drinking all that soda."

"hmmmm, I have been eating a lot of sweets lately, Joanne."

"More cake!"

"The health class teacher told us that when we eat too much sugar, that our

pan cre as

makes the sugar we need to live go too low in our blood.

When that happens is some people get real nervous."

"That's right, honey. And if you have ADHD, like your brother has and OCD, then it is very important to eat the right types of food."

"Mom, stop it! – I don't have any disease."

"OK, dear, then just pretend that you do, for me."

"Fair enough, mom."

"Hmmmmmm, Joey, mom says that I have OCD. Do I, Joey?"

"Well sis,

>You do count those drain grates like you

have to

>You get real weird when you don't find all the things you need for all those collections –

immediately

>And sometimes you **wash your hands** 20

times a day – or at least it
seems that way

I think you do have obsessive-compulsive disorder."

"Who cares what you or mom thinks – I don't care what
you call me."

"Ok, Joanne. I am going to my

neuro feed back session. It helped me a

lot after I got diagnosed with

attention deficit hyperactivity disorder."

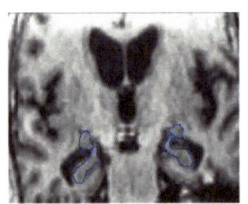

"What the heck is that?"

"Well, they put something on my head and measure how my brain works in different spots. Then get this –

They said  that parts of my
brain works too slow and
other parts are too fast – but I
can learn how to make the fast
parts slower and the slow parts
faster."

16

"How?"

"Well, I change lights, sounds, music that the machine makes by just paying attention to those things – and they say that it helps be 'balance' my brain."

"I hope mom knows about this. They want to know about any practitioners…"

"How did someone know you had ADHD?"

">I was always running around

>I couldn't pay attention

>I was always talking no matter what

>I could never just relax

>I procrastinated all the time

>I never finished anything

>I was easily distracted

>And make lots of careless mistakes – and more.

It's funny, you repeat things because you are different in your way – I repeat things because it sometimes helps me to focus."

"Ok, kids, I'm home. From now on, we are all going to eat really nutritious foods – rich in:

B – complex vitamins

Omega 3 fatty acids

Protein

Calcium

Magnesium

Water"

"Some folks use

supplements."

"I like to get the vitamins and other things right from foods, kids."

"I heard in school, mom, that carbohydrates are important for kids who get nervous too."

"She is right, kiddo - carbs that are not too sweet, like some types of whole grain pasta, can actually help the body make a special chemical that makes us feel relaxed it's called

ser o ton in."

"Mom,
school they
that taking
walk every
can also get
body to
that stuff
that it's
for some
with

in
said
a long
day
the
make
and
good
kids

attention deficit hyperactivity disorder."

"Some kids listen to special music that helps them to relax and some types of music even help some kids to focus," said Joey.

"Well, Joey, I know some kids who take medicine for ADHD."

"Ok, maybe it works for them – they may do whatever they and their parents want to do. Some of them have

side effects."

"Ok, Joey. We get it. Yes people have to think about side effects and all the choices – but their parents have to be involved and it's not ok for you to interfere."

"Whether you take meds or you choose another way, the idea is to make parts of your brain go faster or slower – then you can pay attention better."

"This magazine that some also get if they sit some types artificial light, mom." 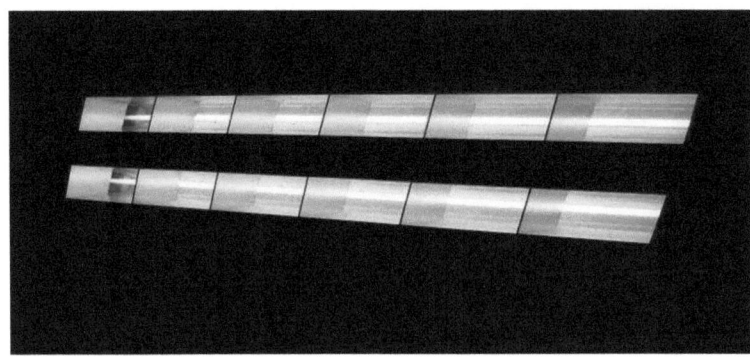 says kids hyper under of

"That's right, Joey."

"Some kids feel better under light that's like the sun and some kids feel real weird under lights that come in long tubes and looks kinda yellowish."

"But some people like light that comes in long tubes that is like the sun."

"OK – and by the way the vitamin D from the sun and all the good things that happen from doing exercise is also good for both of you and dad too – and it's good for my bones too."

"Silly brother, grandpa says that some kid that he knows - his friend's son - gets real hyper when he plays certain video games or just even looks at a computer screen."

"And from artificial colors in food and drinks."

"Yep, them too, I hear you, mom."

"Some kids feel relaxed when they pet animals."

"Keep learning, kids."

"We will mom."

Workbook Section
It's Ok for someone to help with this part!

What are a few things that can make kids more hyper?

1)

2)

3)

4)

5)

What are some things that can help kids to relax?

1)

2)

3)

4)

5)

6)

 What are some signs that someone might have OCD?

1)

2)

3)

4)

5)

Any other ideas?

1)

2)

What are some signs of ADHD?

1)

2)

3)

4)

5)

What are some of the good things that are in foods which are good for both OCD and ADHD?

1)

2)

3)

4)

5)

Please make a list of all the things you eat or drink over a period of a week. Note the days when you feel best as a 1 and the worst a 5.

Day One   Symptoms

Breakfast

Lunch

Dinner

Other

Day Two   Symptoms

Breakfast

Lunch

Dinner

Other

Day Three   Symptom

Breakfast

Lunch

Dinner

Other

<u>Day Four</u>   <u>Symptoms</u>

Breakfast

Lunch

Dinner

Other

<u>Day Five</u>   <u>Symptoms</u>

Breakfast

Lunch

Dinner

Other

<u>Day six</u>   <u>Symptoms</u>

Breakfast

Lunch

Dinner

Other

<u>Day Seven</u>   <u>Symptoms</u>

Breakfast

Lunch

Dinner

Other

Notes:

Notes

www.ingramcontent.com/pod-product-compliance
Lightning Source LLC
Chambersburg PA
CBHW041531280526
45792CB00004B/1458